Who Let the JOY out?

Mark A. Crawford

Wendee,

Blessings.

tower of Joy,
Realized.

Eph 3:20.

M

I dedicate this book to my parents, Ella and Tony Crawford, who both now know the full expression of joy as they experience eternity with their Heavenly Father.

They taught me to never give up and to always finish what I start. Both would be extremely proud to be reading this book.

Thank you to Matthew Groom for the jokes in this book which he obtained from various sources.

I also appreciate very much the editing work done by Annette Crawford and Sid Saxby. Thanks to so many of my friends for encouraging me to write this my second book.

Introduction

IN 2000 A group called the Baha Men released a crazy but catchy song called "Who let the dogs out?" Everyone seemed to be singing it and asking that question. I really do not care who let the dogs out, but I am passionately looking for people who will let the joy out. Charlie Chaplin who lived his life making people laugh said, "A day without laughter is a day wasted." I want to see people being transformed, their lives changed and impacting other lives. I don't like wasted days, months or years.

This book is designed to launch you into a new phase of life and experience of joy by helping you to learn how to experience joy more often.

For many years I quoted and heard others quoting the scripture, "For the joy of the Lord is your strength" and all the time I heard this voice inside of me say "but how, how does the joy of the Lord strengthen me?" especially when the circumstances of life appear anything but joyful.

You are about to find out just how to experience a dimension of joy that has previously been hidden from you. This is where you move from being a responder to things to proactively creating a new environment. This is where you move from theory to experience in a whole new realm of joyfulness. Our responsibility is to realize that our Father in Heaven is seeking our response to His ability.

Over the next thirty days my prayer is that you will establish a habit and practice that transforms your life and the lives of others. So I encourage you to read, meditate and practice each day letting the joy out. Join others for this 30 day experiment and let's create a revolution of joy.

Who Let the Joy Out?

Mark Crawford

Day One

LIFE IS ABOUT exchange!

Today you will be involved in many exchanges. You might exchange conversations with someone else or exchange glances or smiles with another. You will most certainly exchange money for some goods or services. Just like most other days, today is a day of exchanges, and you will hardly realize it; you'll probably not even notice it because you are so used to the exchanges.

Every day, we exchange things we already have for something we want or we need. We find out that we have to let go of what we have in order to receive or obtain what someone else has. Whether it is employment for wages or goods for money, we are daily involved in exchange.

The kingdom of Heaven is also about exchange: exchange of what is yours for the superior things of Heaven. Of course, the choice to exchange is always yours.

You already have an invitation from the Father to receive what Heaven has available for you; you just need to accept that invitation.

You can exchange mourning for dancing, sin for forgiveness, death for life, sickness for health, and abundance for lack. The list goes on and on of the many things that are available to be exchanged.

Today I'm inviting you to make a choice; it's a choice you can get to make every day. This is where you get to say, "I am choosing to exchange today what I have always had for the things of Heaven in my world now."

You can exchange what you presently have in attitude, mind-set, emotional state, and experience for a newfound reality—a reality out of this world.

Today you have this awesome privilege to exchange what you presently carry but do not want in order to receive what you desire but have not yet received.

Throughout this book I will ask a very simple question: "Who let the joy out?"

My prayer and hope is that you'll participate in this exchange and learn to let the joy out.

Go on and give it a try.

Who let the joy out?

Did you hear about the new restaurant on the moon? The food is great, but there's just no atmosphere.

Day Two

REMEMBER LIFE IS about exchange, and so is the kingdom of Heaven.

Today you have the wonderful privilege of being an exchange agent, changing your future and the future of others. You do not have to have what you've always had, for you can have something different.

Deliberately choosing to make an exchange with Heaven will take faith and risk. I encourage you today to refuse to stay the way you are and to reach out for an alternative, something different that will change things forever.

Today you get to either conform to the environment around about you—the status quo, which is the ways things are expected to happen or are usually done—or you can step up and become transformed and therefore be a transformer. Now, that's more than meets the eye.

And do not be conformed to this world, but be transformed by the renewing of your mind, that you may prove what is that good and acceptable and perfect will of God. (Rom. 12:2 NKJV)

Stop imitating the ideals and opinions of the culture around you, but be inwardly transformed by the Holy Spirit through a total reformation of how you think. This will empower you to discern God's will as you live a beautiful life, satisfying and perfect in his eyes. (Rom.12:2, the Passion Translation)

Today, choose the path of transformation. Look at ways to do things differently. Change the route you always take. Style your hair differently. Wear different clothes. Put on a different attitude, and have a grateful day no matter what. Today is your day to change!

Who let the joy out?

I was thinking about moving to Moscow, but there is no point in "Russian" into things.

Day Three

TODAY I WANT you to discover the hidden riches of joy as a power, a force to be reckoned with, a change agent, an atmosphere changer, and a game changer.

Maybe you have heard of the scripture "For the joy of the Lord is your strength" (Neh. 8:10 NKJV). That's the sort of power I am talking about.

In my experience, very few people recognize joy as such a power because they only know joy as an emotion that affects them personally. We all have been taught that joy is something you do as a response to something funny happening that in turn makes you laugh—maybe a comedy show or a good joke. A friend slips on the pavement and does these wonderful acrobatics, without hurting him- or herself, and we laugh about it...after we help our friend up, of course.

When a group of people laugh, we ask, "What are you laughing about?" It is inconceivable and troubling to us that people would be laughing about nothing; there must be something funny to make them laugh. There must be something that causes the laughter. Otherwise you're crazy or weird to laugh at nothing, right?

We generally need to have something to activate joy and laughter—something external to laugh about—and that's how most of us have been trained. Now, I suggest that is more like happiness.

How about laughing right now at nothing? I know it's weird, but you will feel better, feel strengthened, and feel refreshed. Have a go!

Who let the joy out?

If you're struggling to think of what to get your dad for Christmas, then get him a fridge, and watch his face light up when he opens it.

Day Four

MANY YEARS AGO I discovered that the prayer Jesus gave us wasn't just something that He intended to be a quick, easy prayer to be included in a prayer book. After all, He did warn us about praying vain, repetitious prayers. I realized that that He was revealing to us that the will of God was for earth to be Heavenized, and that has led me on a kingdom crusade ever since. I detail more of my thoughts on this in my book *Fascinated by Heaven on Earth*.

Romans 14:17–18 (NKJV) says (emphasis mine), "For the kingdom of God is not eating and drinking, *but righteousness and peace and joy in the Holy Spirit*. For he who serves Christ in these things is acceptable to God and approved by men."

Now, that first part of the verse might be troubling for many of you who enjoy eating as much as I do. However, let me explain from the Passion Translation: "For the kingdom of God is not a matter of rules about food and drink, but is in the realm of the Holy Spirit, filled with righteousness, peace, and joy. Serving the Anointed One by walking in these kingdom realities pleases God and earns the respect of others."

You see, when you live a joyous lifestyle, you bring the kingdom to earth. You please God and earn the respect of others around about you.

Let the kingdom come! Let the joy out today.

Who let the joy out?

I cut my finger shredding cheese, but I think that I may have "grater" problems.

Day Five

SEVERAL YEARS AGO, a study of three thousand people was conducted on behalf of Three Barrels Brandy in the United Kingdom to discover what made people happy. The number one thing that made people happy was finding money in an old pair of jeans. But having a picnic in the sun, getting flowers or chocolates from a loved one, or receiving a thank-you card in the mail were also high on the list.

Sunshine was found to be one of the major factors for happiness. Waking up to a sunny day, sitting in the sun, having a picnic in the sun, and driving with the car windows down on a sunny day all appeared in the top twenty answers.

The study also found that most people feel at their happiest at around six in the evening on Saturdays.

All of these things are external factors that cause a response of happiness or what some would call joy.

Joy is not a response to external factors; it is something you release that affects external things. Joy is not manufactured—it is released. Joy is not produced, but it is released because you have the source of all joy living in you. Joy is an atmosphere changer. Watch what happens when you start to laugh among a group of people; the atmosphere among you changes.

Today, I invite you to intentionally think joy-filled thoughts. Laugh out loud at nothing. I know it sounds weird and will feel weird, *but* you'll feel a whole lot better. You are a joy releaser, and so I ask you today:

Who let the joy out?

Today a girl said she recognized me from vegetarian club, but I'm sure I've never met "herbivore."

Day Six

TODAY LET ME tell you about a significant thought that will help you to enjoy life as you put it into practice and embrace this way of thinking.

There is such a great difference between *facts* and *truth*. Many people confuse the two, giving them the same meanings. Therefore facts become truth, and truth become facts, when in reality there is often a huge difference between them.

The facts are the details of any situation; they are real and demand some attention. We are meant to be aware of the facts. We are not meant to deny them but to instead realize they are not meant to determine our lives.

Truth, on the other hand, is from a superior realm or a different place than the facts. Truth is actually a person: Jesus Christ. He said that He was the way, truth, and life: "Jesus said to him, 'I am the way, the truth, and the life. No one comes to the Father except through Me'" (John 14:6 NKJV).

So truth is what Heaven has to say about your facts, your circumstances, your life, and your future. Often focusing and concentrating on the facts will cause anxiety, worry, and despair. It's when joy is often robbed from you.

However, truth is a place in which joy can abound. It's where joy is welcomed and allowed to expand and operate. Today, be aware of the facts of your situation, but focus on what Heaven has to say about them. Let joy out to dance. Sing and be happy with the truth causing the facts to take their rightful place.

You shall know the truth, and the truth shall set you free.

Who let the joy out today?

I am terrified of elevators. I'm going to start taking steps to avoid them.

Day Seven

WHATEVER YOU ARE facing today, Heaven wants the opportunity to give you a second opinion about the facts you are facing.

You may have been told something about your future based upon some facts, or you may have remembered something from your past based on facts. However, I want you to understand that there is a second opinion available about those facts.

That opinion, which is called the truth, will encourage you, inspire you, and cause you to have joy again in your heart and in your head, and you will be able to release it out of your mouth.

Remember truth is a person, and it is Jesus. He wants to show you what Heaven sees about your facts.

Just ask Him for His second opinion about the facts.

Now, remember the facts are real. They have happened, but you can limit their ability to influence your life and your future. You give authority to the facts or to the truth. You can't change the facts that have happened, but you *can* change how you respond to them.

Just give Heaven an opportunity today to comment on your present reality and to present an alternate future reality that will fill you with hope for the future.

Hope desires to abound in your heart with the partnership of joy. Joy wants to come out of your mouth, releasing a new perspective on those facts and giving you the power to overcome them.

But the new perspective only comes after you step out in faith and release joy into the circumstances. I know you might be crying with sadness or even frustrated with an unsolvable problem. I know that whatever happened can have emotional effects upon you. You may not feel like laughing and releasing joy, but as soon as you do, you will see things change.

Don't let anything keep you from experiencing the truth operating in your life.

Who let the joy out?

Is it you?

A red ship and a blue ship have just collided in the Caribbean. Apparently the survivors are marooned.

Day Eight

REMEMBER THAT THE facts of your life do exist, but you don't have to allow them to have total influence over your life. You can let truth lead you, influence you, and open up a new future for you. Joy loves to partner with truth.

When you acknowledge that there exists an alternative to the facts called "truth," or what Heaven has to say about the facts, then you can begin to discover how to partner with the truth. Partnering with the truth causes you to come into alignment with how Heaven sees your situation and facts. This is a place where you become open to see things from a different perspective and thereby shift your stance. You can become positioned for change and open to see the once-hidden solution to the problem. This is where you begin to look for the good in the situation—not just a positive outlook but the actual presence of Heaven and God in the midst of the situation.

As God works everything together for good then it only seems right that we look for the good in the situations we find ourselves in.

"And we know that all things work together for good to those who love God, to those who are the called according to *His* purpose." (Rom. 8:28 NKJV)

When you start releasing joy you start to see things from Heaven's perspective and see the previously hidden gems in the piles of dirt.

This is where you get to see the facts in the true light of God's love and care for you. This is when you realize that what happened to you was never in His plan for you.

When you see things from a different perspective, you can embrace the truth, and the truth will bring you into freedom. Joy loves truth.

Who let the joy out?

Last night, my wife and I watched three DVDs back to back. Luckily I was the one facing the TV.

Day Nine

DURING THE 1980S German music group Boney M had a hit song "By the Rivers of Babylon." I must admit at that time it was one of my favorite songs. I played it over and over; it did have a catchy tune, and it was the 80s! It was many years later that I realized the words came from the book of Psalms: "By the rivers of Babylon, there we sat down, yea, we wept, when we remembered Zion. We hanged our harps upon the willows in the midst thereof. For there they that carried us away captive required of us a song; and they that wasted us required of us mirth, saying, Sing us one of the songs of Zion. How shall we sing the Lord's song in a strange land?" (Ps. 137:1–4 KJV).

So this passage tells the story of the Israelites, who had been taken captive into Babylon and were so affected by their external circumstances that they could not see a reason to play their music. Even when those around them asked for one of their songs, they just couldn't do it.

They had an opportunity to display God's goodness and His ways to those who had taken them captive. Instead of being overwhelmed by the goodness of God, they were overwhelmed by their circumstances. Instead of display-ing His joy, they decided to display sorrow, sadness, and disappointment. They empowered these feelings to gov-ern them.

I understand how they felt because I have been in many "strange lands," and now I understand that in those lands, Heaven gives me a power to sing when all I feel like doing is crying. All I have to do is step out and begin the song. I usually don't feel like it, but as my wife often reminds me, "What do feelings have to do with it anyway?"

Your "strange land" may just be how you're feeling today. Heaven loves "strange lands" because that is where new songs are birthed and are destined to be sung. There is a power released to sing them; all you need to do is to open your mouth and sing for joy!

Will you let the joy out today?

I fear for the calendar; its days are numbered.

Day Ten

THE IRISH WORSHIP band Blue Tree were invited to play worship music in a bar and brothel in Pattaya, Thailand (a place described as the sex-tourism capital of the world).

They started playing worship music, indeed in a "strange land," when God birthed out of them a new song. That song was a prophetic sound that came out as they sang. Chris Tomlin made the song "God of this City" famous. This song, birthed in a very dark place, has become a prophetic declaration for many cities across the nations.

The challenge always comes to us to make a choice in what we will allow to determine our day and our future. One choice will often end up robbing us, and the other will empower us. Choosing to release joy will change your day by empowering you and your life.

A couple listened to me teaching this in Sheridan, Wyoming. They left the meeting and went home and decided to release joy into an area in which they needed a breakthrough. They wanted to sell their home. They had tried and had not been successful. No doubt they were discouraged. So they laughed at the situation and then went to bed. When they woke the next morning, the Realtor called them. They had a new buyer who offered an unconditional contract and who was prepared to pay above the asking price. Coincidence? I don't think so; this was an example of the power of joy to change things.

Today, will you make a choice and let joy out?

Who let the joy out?

There are two cannibals eating a clown. One of the cannibals says, "Doesn't this taste funny to you?"

Day Eleven

ONE OF THE most powerful lies that people believe today is that we don't have a choice about life. Heaven declares that there is always a choice available for you to make about your life. Sometimes it seems like it is not much of a choice, but it's still a choice.

Unfortunately many people believe that they simply have to put up with the way things are because there is no alternative and certainly no ability to make a choice for something different. They think that everything is already programmed, and we are just walking it out like robots or puppets. Maybe that is because that is how they experienced life, so they think that's how it will always be.

A powerful truth for you today is that you can choose something different. Take a deep breath, and say out aloud, "I *can* choose. I c-a-n choose!"

Joy is a choice. Is that a surprise to you? Well, then let me tell you that today, you can choose to have joy.

I wonder if you have ever even dared to consider that joy is a choice. Paul declared this several times, and in one verse in Philippians, he emphasizes it: "Rejoice in the Lord always. Again I will say, rejoice!" (4:4 NKJV). He was saying have joy again, go on have joy again.

The passion translation says, "Be cheerful with joyous celebration in every season of life. Let joy overflow, for you are united with the Anointed One!"

Make a choice right now: let joy out.

Who let the joy out?

I'm giving away all my dead batteries today, free of charge.

Day Twelve

LET JOY OVERFLOW! You can allow joy to overflow; you can choose to have joy overflowing just the same way you can choose to let your kitchen sink overflow by intentionally turning on the tap with the plug in the outlet and letting it flow.

So if Paul says that we are to rejoice—that is, we are to have joy again—then we must be able to choose to release joy. For there is no sense in telling people to do something when there is no ability or power to do it. That is sadistic and unreasonable.

In fact in Philippians 3:1 from the Passion Translation, Paul says, "My beloved ones, don't ever limit your joy or fail to rejoice in the wonderful experience of knowing our Lord Jesus! I don't mind repeating what I've already written you because it protects you."

Again, he is saying that we can limit our joy, and therefore we can also have unlimited joy too. Whenever the Bible tells you to do something, God always makes available to you the power to accomplish that thing.

So what will it be today? More of the same? Or will you choose to risk looking foolish and begin to let joy out of your mouth?

Who let the joy out in your world? Ha-ha!

www.Conjunctivitis.com—now that's a site for sore eyes.

Day Thirteen

TODAY LET ME share with you a life-changing thought about joy.

Get ready.

Here it is! Joy is a catalyst.

A catalyst is some agent or action that produces a reaction or acceleration. The catalyst is unaffected, but the substance is changed. A catalyst is often used in chemistry. It can also be activity by a person or thing that precipitates an event or change. We have seen people whose talk, enthusiasm, or energy causes others to be more friendly, enthusiastic, or energetic.

A catalyst is wonderful and powerful but of little use until it comes into contact with the substance it will react with. It must leave the container and come into direct contact with the substance to cause the reaction. It's not until the catalyst does its job of simply being present that it produces the reaction that everyone is looking for. The catalyst does little more than assist unreactive substances to react together. The substances do the reacting; the catalyst affects the rate that they react together.

Without a catalyst, the substances would not react together, or only very slowly. So the catalyst affects things but is not itself affected or used up.

While the catalyst stays in the safe and secure place of its hiding, then there is no change, no reaction, no acceleration—just the same old, same old.

While you keep the catalyst of joy inside of you, it will not bring about the reaction you so need. You need to let the catalyst of joy out of the container of *you*.

Today you can create a life-changing reaction and let the joy out!

Who let the joy out?

A sandwich walks into a bar. The bartender says, "Sorry, we don't serve food here."

Day Fourteen

JOY IS A catalyst for endurance.

Hebrews 12:1–2 (NKJV) says, "Therefore we also, since we are surrounded by so great a cloud of witnesses, let us lay aside every weight, and the sin which so easily ensnares us, and let us run with endurance the race that is set before us, looking unto Jesus, the author and finisher of our faith, who for the joy that was set before Him endured the cross, despising the shame, and has sat down at the right hand of the throne of God."

In the first verse, it tells us what we need to do, and the second verse tells us how to do it. To run with endurance must be something we receive from Heaven; if it's something we do in our own strength, then we must be able to save ourselves too. Life is not meant to be about trying harder in order to change. It's about letting go and taking up things that empower us.

Jesus demonstrated that enduring the cross was possible because of joy. The cross was anything but joyous. It was a horrendous experience. But it was joy that enabled Jesus to continue through this most unimaginable pain. It enabled Him to totally reject shame and to refuse to feel ashamed.

This same endurance is yours when you use the catalyst of joy to produce it.

So when you release joy and have need of endurance, it will cause endurance to turn up to manifest itself. Does it sound too good to be true? Then it must be God, because He is too good.

Go on—try it. I dare you!

Who let the joy out today?

Patient: "Doctor, I've broken my arm in several places."

Doctor: "Well, don't go to those places."

Day Fifteen

JOY IS A catalyst to hope. "Now may the God of hope fill you with all joy and peace in believing, that you may abound in hope by the power of the Holy Spirit" (Rom. 15:13 NKJV).

Now, I just need to remind you that hope is *not* just another word for "wishful thinking." It's a much more intentional word that means an earnest, confident expectation for good. It's about anticipation. So it's a power word.

Where there is hope, there is life.

Hope is also something that God wants to abound in your life because it also empowers faith, and faith is the substance of something hoped for. When you operate your life in faith, you please God, so it's pretty important.

Being filled with joy will help you to believe that you can abound in hope by the power of the Holy Spirit. Your intentional act of releasing joy will cause a catalytic effect on hope, producing more of it—so much more that you have plenty to give away to family, friends, and anyone else who needs some more hope in his or her life.

There is no doubt that the world needs more hope, as there are strong expressions of hopelessness everywhere. You have the key in your hand today to release the catalyst of joy into your world that will cause a reaction and acceleration of hope.

Today, are you a producer of hope and letting the joy out?

Who let the joy out?

Why do crabs never give to charity?

Because they're "shellfish."

Day Sixteen

THERE SEEMS TO me to be a catalyst-type link between joy and abundance. God told His people in Deuteronomy that He was very unhappy with the way they served Him. "He said, 'Because you did not serve the LORD your God with joy and gladness of heart, *for the abundance of everything*, therefore you shall serve your enemies, whom the LORD will send against you, in hunger, in thirst, in nakedness, and in need of everything; and He will put a yoke of iron on your neck until He has destroyed you'" (Deut. 28:47–48 NKJV, emphasis mine).

Perhaps He was also saying that serving Him in joy and gladness caused abundance in their lives. They did not live lives that displayed that joy and gladness in celebration for the abundance available to them and thus realize that abundance was available. Instead, they believed the lie of lack and lived lives that were dominated by the reality of lack rather than the truth of abundance. He expected them to realize that His nature was that of abundance and wanted them to understand that in serving Him, they could partake of that abundance through understanding that there was abundance. He wanted them to celebrate that truth.

However, most likely they lived life complaining about the lack, the temporary circumstances they found themselves in. Then because of their choice, they got to spend more time with that choice—the choice of lack. This displayed to others a wrong perspective of who God really is. They displayed a distorted image of what it looks like to serve God. He was saying because you misrepresented Me to the people around about you and because you misrepresented that My kingdom is a kingdom of lack, then I will let you serve the one you spoke about all the time. I will give you over to whom you recognized and celebrated. I will give you your choice and let you serve your enemy and your desire.

Do you see how vital it is for you to acknowledge abundance and let the joy out?

Who let the joy out?

I went to the doctor and said, "One moment I feel like I am a teepee, and the next moment I feel like I am a wigwam."

"Oh, I see," said the doctor. "I think you are 'two tents.'"

Day Seventeen

"THE JOY OF the Lord is your strength" (Neh. 8:10 NKJV). This well-known scripture was declared by Nehemiah as a result of the reaction of Israel when the public reading of scripture was reintroduced after many years of silence.

He was declaring that joy comes from God and that joy is a strengthener. It also provides an ability to keep on keeping on, to persevere.

David said in the Old Testament, "I would have lost heart, unless I had believed that I would see the goodness of the LORD in the land of the living. Wait on the LORD; be of good courage, and He shall strengthen your heart; wait, I say, on the LORD!" (Ps. 27:13–14 NKJV).

He would have fainted, given up, and said, "That's it. I've had enough—no more." But the goodness of God revitalizes a person and enables correct perspective of the situation and the future.

Focusing on the goodness of God in the land and place you are living will take you into a place where you can release that joy, for the joy of the Lord is your strength today. Look among your circumstances today, and see where goodness is hiding. You must be able to find something to give thanks for.

God works all things together for good! He is good, and He wants to show you His nature. He wants you to realize His presence and to look for it among the circumstances of today.

When you intentionally release joy, then it attracts supernatural strength into your being. It's like bees to a honey pot or metal filings to a magnet. When joy is released, strength from Heaven cannot resist coming to you.

So will you let the joy out today?

Who let the joy out?

What do snowmen do in their spare time?

Just chill.

Day Eighteen

HAVE YOU EVER noticed that sometimes when you have to do something important, you often don't feel like doing it? Something that will build you up and encourage you seems so difficult to do. But when you finally do it, a breakthrough moment seems to occur. You may also find yourself asking why you didn't do that sooner.

This is what is often referred to as operating in the "opposite spirit" or the "opposite way." Others refer to it as "spiritual warfare" because you are warring against what you don't want to do and what you need to do.

I often say to people that when you least feel like reading the Word of God, that's when you most need to do it. While it's not the only time, it is usually the most important time. It's the same with physical exercise. When you least feel like doing it, that's when you seem to benefit the most when you do it.

Several years ago I was in Pakistan with a team of Australians teaching leaders about the Holy Spirit and ministering to them.

After a very exhausting travel through the country, we arrived at the capital, Islamabad. When I woke up the next morning, I could not get out of bed, as my body ached all over. All my joints seemed to have frozen and were painful. I was effectively paralyzed. The team came into the room and started praying. After a little while, the team leader began to laugh for no apparent reason. I wasn't impressed that he was laughing at a situation that was far from joyful for me. One by one the rest of the team started laughing, and then finally I was too. That laughter and joy broke the condition, and I was immediately healed.

Joy is an amazing weapon, and when you fire it, things change.

In 2 Corinthians 10:4 (NKJV), it says, "For the weapons of our warfare are not carnal but mighty in God for pulling down strongholds."

A carnal weapon looks like a weapon. Therefore a weapon that is "not carnal" would not look like a weapon. Joy is one of the weapons this passage is referring to. Joy is a major weapon for you to use against strongholds in thinking and the spiritual realm.

You just have to use the weapon. Your enemy hates joy; he will run from it as quickly as he can.

Will you make an intentional decision today to let the joy out?

Who let the joy out?

Apparently taking a day off is not something you should do when you work for a calendar company.

Day Nineteen

WHEN THE ISRAELITES began to possess the Promised Land, they were given a strategy on how to take the first city, Jericho. It was a strange set of instructions that proved to be powerful.

They were to march around the city once each day for six days without saying anything. Now, that's a miracle in itself; these people, when they went into the wilderness for forty years, did little but complain. Now they must keep quiet. They must wait for the appointed time before they let anything out of their mouth.

Then on the seventh day, they were to go around six times, again keeping quiet. Then the seventh time, they were to let out a shout and blow the trumpets.

The Hebrew word that is used for "shout" means, among other things, to make a joyful noise or to shout for joy, and so they were to release from their mouths joy. They were to let joy out.

There is often a reference to shouting for joy in the scripture as a response to God's greatness. So they let out the greatness of God in a joy-filled manner that created a destructive force for good. The walls of the city came tumbling down. Their inheritance was revealed. The things that kept them from their inheritance, those impenetrable walls, became like nothing to them.

It does seem that when you let joy out as a shout, it has a declarative effect upon things and enables you to step through obstacles, oppositions, and impossible walls. Releasing joy destroys the obstructions between you and your destiny. It makes a way where there seems to be no way.

Go ahead and make your day—try it out. It will make things change around you. Go ahead and let the joy out.

Who let the joy out?

Which country's capital is the fastest growing?

Ireland's. Every year it's "Dublin."

Day Twenty

EACH OF US sees things in a particular way according to how we have lived life and how we have been influenced by parents, friends, and others. Many things throughout your life have also shaped your worldview. When I am in the United States, people there think I have an accent. Now, I don't think I do; I think they are the ones with the accent.

The reality is that we all see with an "accent," or a particular perspective, paradigm, or way of solving a problem. That perspective changes over time too.

However, there are days when the perspective is particularly dark or clouded—so clouded we can find it hard to see where we are going. To see truth apart from the reality of the facts, to understand life through emotional states, or to just see the solution for some situation we are facing can be very difficult.

When you release joy, it seems to attack the cloudiness of wrong perspective. It shifts your focus from the problem to the solution. It attracts Heaven and the attitude of Heaven. You begin to see things as Heaven sees them.

You involve Heaven in your events; you bring Heaven to earth; you receive a Heavenly "accent."

It has the effect that wind has on fog, blowing it away and revealing what's always been there. It reveals the truth in the midst of dark, confusing, and opposing circumstances.

In reality you have been given your Heavenly accent, and now you're able to see the same set of circumstances from Heaven's perspective. Joy is able to flow despite the facts of your circumstances.

Who let the joy out?

A panda walks into a bar and says to the bartender, "I'll have a Scotch and...Coke, thank you."

"Sure thing," the bartender replies and asks, "but what's with the big pause?"

The panda holds up his hands and says, "I was born with them."

Day Twenty-One

IT DOES NOT take much reading or understanding to realize that God is very, very generous, and His nature is abundance.

Actually, I am writing this while sitting in a café, in Hobart, Tasmania, called Abundance. God's nature is abundant, and in fact it is over-the-top abundant. His response to the love He has for this world was to give His son as a sacrifice. God is an outrageous giver who delights in out-giving us. I think for Him, it's an exciting competition.

So in Ephesians 3:20 (NKJV), we see a description of the nature of His heart to be excessive, to be superabundant in all He does: "So let each one give as he purposes in his heart, not grudgingly or of necessity; for God loves a cheerful giver" (2 Cor. 9:7 NKJV).

God loves a person who is intentionally giving with a cheerful or hilarious attitude and position. That is a person who gives in an attitude of cheerfulness or hilarity is one who is going to please God.

For most people giving money away for anything is often more like a horror story rather than a comedy time. We are so trained to feel like giving equals losing something rather than being equal investment. When we give, we are commanded to expect a return. No farmer would sow a crop of corn and then forget about it because he never expected to actually get a crop at all. That's a ludicrous situation.

So you cannot expect a return from an investment of nothing. When you need to make a withdrawal, there needs to be something in the bank to withdraw. Investing financially in the kingdom is not an option. You get to choose which way you will invest.

Learn how to release joy. Letting joy out when you least need it will provide joy for you when you most need joy to impact your life.

Today would be a good day to sow seeds—seeds of joy.

Who let the joy out?

I needed a password eight characters long, so I picked Snow White and the Seven Dwarfs.

Day Twenty-Two

DO YOU REMEMBER the song from the 1980s by Bobby McFerrin called "Don't Worry; Be Happy"? It was a catchy, simple sound that everyone seemed to be singing around that time.

Here's the first verse:

> "Here's a little song I wrote
> You might want to sing it note for note
> Don't worry, be happy
> In every life we have some trouble
> But when you worry you make it double
> Don't worry, be happy!" (www.azlyrics.com)

Nothing seems to rob joy from your life like worry. I think it's why Jesus taught on it because the operation of worry in your life robs not only joy but so many other valuable kingdom natures from you.

So Bobby McFerrin was on to something when he penned this simple little ditty. He was also saying what Jesus taught. If you worry about things, it's as unproductive as sitting in a rocking chair: it's all action, but you just don't go anywhere. Instead, be happy and release joy from your life into the circumstances—the same circumstances that were creating the worry—and that will change things.

Your perspective will change; your emotional state will be uplifted. Everything will seem different. You will turn from just surviving into a life of thriving.

"Don't worry; be happy."

Who let the joy out?

How do you organize a space party? You "planet."

Day Twenty-Three

PROVERBS 3:5–6 (NKJV) declares that we ought to trust the Lord with all of our hearts and minds and acknowledge Him in all our ways. Whatever we acknowledge, become aware of, comprehend, declare, discover, or understand, then those things will guide the way in which we walk.

So whatever you acknowledge will determine how you live. For instance, if fear is something that you acknowledge, dwell on, and unconsciously give leadership of your life to, it will determine the decisions you make, the places you go and the people you interact with. The fear then sets the boundaries of your life in a way that removes you from trusting God and Heaven. That's because you are looking for fear and not for faith decisions. You're trying to find reasons why something will not work rather than for ways to make something work and succeed. In fact you now have more faith in the devil than in God. See how easily things change?

In my book *Fascinated by Heaven on Earth*, I write about the reticular activator system (RAS), which is a part of our brain that helps us filter out the billions of pieces of information we receive every day. It functions as an editor to sort through all that information.

For instance, imagine you are looking for a new car—say a red Mazda 6. You take it for a test drive and are very interested in its performance. You take it back to the showroom and leave to think about the deal. While driving along the freeway, you pass several red Mazda 6 sedans. In fact, they are all over the place! They must have suddenly appeared. No, they were there all the time, but your reticular activator is now looking for them.

Whatever you look for, you will find it! Whatever you acknowledge, it will direct your path.

Many Christians seem to be focused on excess; that is, they fear doing things that may look like excess. They look at something that might challenge them and call it excess. They therefore also fear going into abundance. I want to fear lack more than I am concerned about excess; I want to acknowledge and let abundance guide my walk rather than an attribute of hell called "lack." Whatever you acknowledge *will* direct your path.

Let me say that again: whatever you acknowledge will direct your path. So today are you acknowledging that you are a joy carrier and therefore letting the joy out?

Who let the joy out?

Did you hear about the two silk worms in a race? It ended in a tie.

Day Twenty-Four

GOD HAS DESIGNED and put within our DNA ability for us to magnify things. Therefore we can't help ourselves from doing just that—magnifying things—whether we realize it or not.

When you magnify something, you make it appear bigger than what it really is. You increase the apparent size of it; you don't actually make it bigger, but it can feel like it.

Now, of course we know we are meant to magnify the Lord at all times. When we don't, we will magnify something else: the problem, the circumstances, our doubts, and our worries.

The problem arises when we fail to magnify Him.

So remember that when something is magnified, it appears bigger than it really is.

When we magnify the Lord in the midst of circumstances, we invite His nature and presence into our present reality. Joy becomes present, and it is far easier to see the solution than to remain problem focused. We become empowered to release the joy of the Lord and His strength.

When we magnify the circumstances, worry, focus on the problem, or partner with anxiety, then we actually are magnifying something we ought not to. In fact, we have created an idol we are worshipping. We will be overcome with the extent of what we are magnifying. We will be overwhelmed by the problem and far from being able to see the answer.

Light can be magnified in strength by focusing the light. In the same way, focusing on Him, His strength, and His nature and not the circumstances will enable you to have Heaven's perspective on the circumstances.

When you let joy out, you are releasing an attribute of the Father. You are bringing His presence into your circumstances and enabling yourself to magnify Him.

Who let the joy out?

What do you call a group of killer whales playing instruments?

An "orca-stra."

Day Twenty-Five

FAITH IS SAID to be the currency of Heaven, and therefore it activates and unlocks things. It's the act of faith that releases things that are present but not yet manifest.

Hebrews 11:6 says, "And without faith living within us it would be impossible to please God. For we come to God in faith knowing that he is real and that he rewards the faith of those who truly seek him." (NKJV)

Joy is faith activated.

It doesn't matter whether you feel like it or feel weak or feel strong or feel lost or all powerful. It's not a matter of feelings but an intentional act to release joy. Sometimes it takes more intentionality than at other times, but it still takes faith.

It's like putting the key into the ignition of the car, which is so often an unconscious but faith-filled action:

you start the vehicle and drive away. Just sitting there with the keys in your hand will get you nowhere.

When you use that faith, it greatly pleases God. His greatest pleasure is for His children to believe His word and act upon it.

We all have been given a measure of faith, and when you use that measure, it becomes more faith. It is not exhausted by use; it's actually increased.

The greatest pleasure you can give God is to believe His word; without faith, it is impossible to please Him. (Heb. 11:6 NKJV)

Today, take hold of faith, and release joy out of your mouth.

Who let the joy out?

I just watched a documentary about beavers...it was the best "dam" program I've ever seen.

Day Twenty-Six

GOD HAS ALREADY introduced Himself as a Father, but not just any father—our Father who is in Heaven. Your Father who wants his children living a life in relationship with Him.

Prior to coming into relationship with our Heavenly Father, we were spiritually orphans. Whether we realized that or not, we were. We were all separated from God; independent, rebellious and lonely.

So we need to be born again and enter into a new life and no longer be actual spiritual orphans; I hope you already know that experience and have become part of the family of God. If not, then right now, you can ask God, and it will happen faster than you realize—it's that easy. There are no special words just your desire to become part of the family that you vocalize to Him.

While so much in our lives changes by being born again, we still all have thinking that wants to take us back into behaving like an orphan or a victim. This sort of thinking is more confined to believing that you are not worthy to access things in Heaven; that you need someone, preferably God, to do things for you; and that you need to have someone to blame if it doesn't work.

Maturity is living life taking responsibility for your actions and your future. Responsibility is really your response to your father in Heavens ability. It's time to throw away the blame game. It's time to stop waiting for God to do something and take a step to initiate something new in your life.

When you understand who you really are and live from a son-of-God mind-set, you will move from being reactive to being a leader, being an initiator, and becoming proactive. Every time you intentionally and purposefully let joy out of your life, then you are developing your proactive, victorious life.

Joy reinforces your sonship and defeats the victim mind-set.

Who let the joy out today?

Breaking news! Energizer Bunny arrested—charged with battery.

Day Twenty-Seven

IF YOU DEVELOP a lifestyle of releasing joy and therefore develop a stronghold of joy in your life, then you will see things from a different positive perspective than most others will. The world about you takes on different meaning.

Yes, I said a stronghold of joy. There are negative wrong strongholds in people's lives but they should be positive strongholds you are building; Heavens stronghold in your life.

If you don't develop this joy, then you will look for happiness or your type of joy from other things. You're more likely to find addictions to other things that will comfort you rather than experience true joy.

C. S. Lewis said that "joy is the serious business of Heaven." While seriousness is not a fruit of the Spirit, Joy is a fruit of the Spirit; that is, the activity of the Holy Spirit in your life.

James tells us that we are to "count it all joy when you fall into various trials" (James 1:2 NKJV). That's part of the serious business of joy. The Greek meaning of the word "count" is to be in command, lead, or to be chief of. So therefore I suggest that we are to let joy be in command or to lead our response or to be the chief emotion in difficult situations that we would see as trials.

This is what we would also call operating in the opposite spirit, or spiritual warfare. When we come into trials, and that's inevitable, then we are to laugh at the circumstances and let joy have command of our feelings.

Today are you letting joy out. Remember it's the serious business of Heaven.

Who let the joy out?

My dog used to chase people on a bike a lot. It got so bad that I finally had to take his bike away.

Day Twenty-Eight

COUNTLESS STUDIES HAVE shown a direct link between laughter, joy, and healing. The Robin Williams movie *Patch Adams* showed how laughter and humor can aid the healing process. The character Patch Adams hit resistance from the established medical profession because they were more concerned treating the illness than the person.

Long ago, Proverbs revealed that laughter was powerful and healing to a person. Those same studies have confirmed that truth. "A joyful, cheerful heart brings healing to both body and soul, but the one whose heart is crushed struggles with sickness and depression" (Prov. 17:22, the Passion Translation).

So as you let the joy out, it releases a healing power. It sets your body into a position to experience and receive healing. Laughing release endorphins, which are like nature's natural painkillers, and they create a feeling and sense of well-being.

As a practitioner of joy here is my prescription for you today, it is to take your medicine at least three times a day, with or without food. So laugh at least three times a day and see what changes. Go on take your medicine.

It seems to me that this is another catalyst that, when released, causes a reaction.

Laughter is the best medicine, with no negative side effects.

Who let the joy out?

In a boomerang shop: "I'd like to buy a new boomerang, please. Also, can you tell me how to throw the old one away?"

Day Twenty-Nine

JESUS, IN TALKING to His disciples one day, told them that in order for them to see the kingdom of Heaven, then they had to behave like children. He was telling them to be childlike, not childish.

While children are playing, you will usually hear lots of laughter. In fact most parents know something is wrong if it goes quiet or there is crying. But as long as there is laughter, everything is all right.

Jesus was telling us that in order to see the kingdom as He wanted us to see it, we needed to behave like little children. Many of us have matured so much that we have grown out of joy and taken hold of seriousness to an extended level.

It is childlike to laugh at something that has no basis for being funny. It's childlike to laugh for no reason at all. That's what Jesus was trying to get us to do—experience the laugh of delight, the laugh of a child. "Delight yourself also in the Lord, and He shall give you the desires of your heart" (Ps. 37:4).

Now, remember that paradox must be your friend. You must realize that Jesus used it so often. Paradox is when two competing truths come together. So we are to be childlike with laughter and giggle about nothing and behave like a child would and yet also be forceful and take the kingdom as a warrior would. The two seem totally incompatible, and yet the Holy Spirit brings those two powerful concepts together to work as one.

Remember Jesus did not tell us to be childish or immature in our behavior, like children fighting over the toys in the same playpen. Growing up means keeping things from our childhood instead of throwing them away as most of us have done. Imagination, delight, and joy are powerful things to keep.

Who let the joy out?

I can't believe I forgot to go to the gym today. That's seven years in a row now.

Day Thirty

STING SINGS A song that echoes in my head often: "Every breath you take, every move you make, every bond you break, every step you take I'll be watching you. Every single day, every word you say, every game you play, every night you stay I'll be watching you. Oh, can't you see you belong to me, how my poor heart aches with every step you take..." (www.azlyrics.com)

While I don't think this song was written in the way I want to interpret it, I truly think it easily fits into the nature of God. So look at again at the lyrics as if your Father in Heaven were singing them to you.

"Every breath you take, every move you make, every bond you break, every step you take I'll be watching you. Every single day, every word you say, every game you play, every night you stay I'll be watching you. Oh, can't you see you belong to me, how my poor heart aches with every step you take..." (www.azlyrics.com)

Now, He is never watching you to see if you make a mistake or sin. He is watching to see how He can partner with you and how He can bring more joy to you and through you. He is joyfully watching every move you make.

David knew of this thought, which is why he wrote in Psalm 16:11 that in God's presence is the fullness of joy. It's understandable, isn't it? Since joy begins and ends in God, then when we experience His presence, we experience great joy. That's why in some meetings where the presence of God is so strong, people start to be overcome by joy and laughter, and it refreshes people because in His presence is the fullness of joy.

In the New Testament, Pentecost brought this out in Acts 2:28 (NKJV): "You have made known to me the ways of life; You will make me full of joy in your presence."

When you let the joy out, you can be sure that God will cause His presence to be experienced.

Who let the joy out?

A patient bursts into a doctor's office. "Doctor, I believe I'm a deck of cards!"

The doctor calmly replies, "Go sit in the waiting room, please; I'll be dealing with you later."

Day Thirty-One

I HAVE A simple, uncomplicated question to ask you today.

Who let the joy out today?

Made in the USA
Monee, IL
29 September 2024

66242201R00056